P9-CQP-972

BASIC ESSENTIALS™
SOLO HIKING

DISCARDED BY

MT. LEBANON PUBLIC LIBRARY

Mt. Lebanon Public Library
16 Castle Shannon Boulevard
Pittsburgh, Pennsylvania 15228

Help Us Keep This Guide Up to Date

Every effort has been made by the author and editors to make this guide as accurate and useful as possible. However, many things can change after a guide is published—new products and information become available, regulations change, techniques evolve, etc.

We would love to hear from you concerning your experiences with this guide and how you feel it could be improved and be kept up to date. While we may not be able to respond to all comments and suggestions, we'll take them to heart and we'll also make certain to share them with the author. Please send your comments and suggestions to the following address:

The Globe Pequot Press
Reader Response/Editorial Department
P.O. Box 833
Guilford, CT 06437

Or you may e-mail us at:

editorial@globe-pequot.com

Thanks for your input, and happy travels!

BASIC ESSENTIALS™ SERIES

BASIC ✳ ESSENTIALS™

SOLO HIKING

ADRIENNE HALL

The Globe Pequot Press

Guilford, Connecticut

Copyright © 2002 by The Globe Pequot Press

All rights reserved. No part of this book may be reproduced or transmitted in any form by any means, electronic or mechanical, including photocopying and recording, or by any information storage and retrieval system, except as may be expressly permitted by the 1976 Copyright Act or by the publisher. Requests for permission should be made in writing to The Globe Pequot Press, P.O. Box 480, Guilford, Connecticut 06437.

Basic Essentials is a registered trademark of The Globe Pequot Press.

Cover photo by EyeWire
Cover design by Lana Mullen
Text and layout design by Casey Shain
Illustrations by Diane Blasius

Many thanks to the following companies and individuals for providing photos: pp. 6, 20, and 22: Mountain Safety Research; pp. 7 and 10: Mountain Hardwear; pp. 9, 12 top, 12 bottom, and 26: Kelty; pp. 12 middle, 13, 15 background, 24 middle, and 24 bottom: Lisa Reneson; p. 15 top left: Lowa Boots; p. 15 top right: Asolo USA, Inc.; and pp. 15 bottom and 23: Outdoor Research. All other photos are by the author.

Library of Congress Cataloging-in-Publication Data
Hall, Adrienne.
   Basic essentials. Solo hiking / Adrienne Hall. —1st ed.
     p. cm. — (Basic essentials series)
   ISBN: 0-7627-0956-1
    1. Hiking. 2. Backpacking. I. Title.

GV199.5.H34 2001
796.51—dc21

MT. LEBANON PUBLIC LIBRARY

MAR 2 2 2002

♻ Printed on recycled paper
Manufactured in the United States of America
First Edition/First Printing

The Globe Pequot Press assumes no liability for accidents happening to, or injuries sustained by, readers who engage in the activities described in this book.

Contents

Introduction

There are many things to love about hiking: the way your stride strengthens under the weight of your pack; the way the sticky smell of a pine forest reminds you to inhale completely; the way, after a few days out, you begin to lose yourself to the landscape and acquire a sense of serenity, balance, and vigor. It is for these reasons and many others that millions of people around the world turn their backs on bustling towns, slip into tough-soled boots, and head for the hills. Whether you spend two hours hiking the rolling Appalachian countryside or two weeks tramping around the jagged peaks of the North Cascades, you'll discover the rewards of spending time in wild places.

Quite possibly you've done most of your backcountry traveling with others. But maybe the logistics and social aspects of group travel have lost their appeal. With your limited vacation schedule, perhaps it is too difficult to find a compatible hiking partner. Or maybe you've decided that the quiet sounds of nature would be preferable to your buddy's huffing and puffing as he follows your footsteps up each hill. You'd like to sprawl out in your tent at night and have the decision of how to spend each day be entirely your own. If you're considering hiking solo for the first time, or if you've already ventured out on your own, this book will help you feel more prepared and confident in your solo travels. Whatever the case may be, I'm glad you're here, thinking about going solo.

Opportunities for solitude and adventure abound for the solo hiker.

Whether you choose to take an afternoon walk in the woods or spend a week in the backcountry, when you go alone you engage in an intimate interaction with your surroundings, one that would be quite difficult to experience when traveling with others. Solo hikers have a better chance of experiencing such characteristics of wilderness as solitude, natural quiet, and a feeling of detachment from civilization. Without the distractions of social interactions, you commune more completely with nature. Whether your communion involves meditating on a grassy mountaintop or hooking a ten-pound trout is entirely up to you, but most solo hikers return from the backcountry with a deep peace and a sense of self-discovery. Hiking solo provides time for introspection. It brings you face to face with the real you and forces you to be accountable for your actions. Backcountry skills improve when it's up to you to cook all the meals, secure adequate shelter, and find the route. Indeed, it is a terrific way to challenge yourself.

As a solo hiker you also have a better chance of observing wildlife: Bambi is less likely to bolt from a quiet solo trekker than from an army of Boy Scouts clambering up the trail. Feel free to travel at your own pace, stop for breaks, take pictures whenever you like, design your own route, determine your daily mileage, and choose your own campsite. Solo hikers eliminate the potential for conflict with a hiking partner, and they're never kept awake at night by a snoring tentmate!

While the benefits of solo travel are numerous, you should also recognize that solo trips come with their own set of challenges. You will not have a companion with whom you can laugh or wait out a storm. Upon returning to civilization, many solo hikers feel that they have a big secret that no one else can understand. There are also a number of safety issues associated with solo travel. It is not my job, however, to discourage you or to scare you into staying home. My job is to make you aware of the differences between solo and shared travel and to teach you how to deal with the risks inherent in going solo. My job is to provide you with the skills and knowledge you need to have a safe and enjoyable time in wild places and to know how to prevent dangerous situations or deal with one should it arise. Yes, there are risks. But I imagine that you understand there are risks involved in most things worthwhile in life. If the idea of sleeping alone in the dark woods scares you, know that flirting with your fears often ends up teaching you something important about yourself.

That said, this book focuses on aspects of hiking that are unique to solo travelers. Going solo is different from hiking with others in two major ways: (1) You, and only you, carry and use all the equipment; and (2) you must contend with a number of risks inherent in solo travel. The first part of this book will help you make informed choices about

MT. LEBANON PUBLIC LIBRARY

backpacking gear for a solo trip and will make sure you'll be able to carry and use your gear when you're out there on your own. The second part of the book will teach you how to deal with difficult situations, such as inclement weather, animals, and medical emergencies, and how to stay safe and healthy when you're by yourself.

One more thing: People—most often friends and family—may tell you you're crazy for wanting to spend days and nights by yourself in the wilderness. Your mother will insist that you take your little brother. Aunt Judy may start praying. If you're a woman, expect people to cringe, shake their heads with worry, and ask what weapons you'll be carrying for protection. Hear them out, for they probably mean well. Tactfully decline Uncle Ted's .22 Beretta, then be on your way—they have no idea what they're missing!

Packing *for a* Solo Trip

T he first logical question after deciding to embark on a solo trip is "What should I take?" And the logical answer to that question is "It depends where you're going." At the end of this section are two checklists, one for a dayhike and one for a backpacking trip. You won't need to take every item on the lists (for example, it would be silly to take insect repellent on a winter trip). Choose gear that is appro-priate for the place through which you'll be traveling and for the time of year. While taking items like a journal, camera, or guidebook is a matter of personal preference, other pieces of equipment will come with you on every backcountry excursion. These essential gear items warrant special considerations for the solo hiker, so that's what we'll talk about now.

Shelter

There are three options for shelter, all of which can work well for the solo hiker. The most popular and most comfortable option is a one-person tent. These tents roll into a small bundle and can weigh less than three pounds. For maximum living space and protection from the elements, a tent is the way to go.

The savvy soloist will choose a tent wisely: You certainly don't need to lug a twelve-pound bomb-proof shelter up Knee Knocker Ridge. Weight, of course, is an important consideration. So is the tent's design. Does the tent have a vestibule; that is, a sheltered space outside the tent door that is created by the rainfly? Is the vestibule large

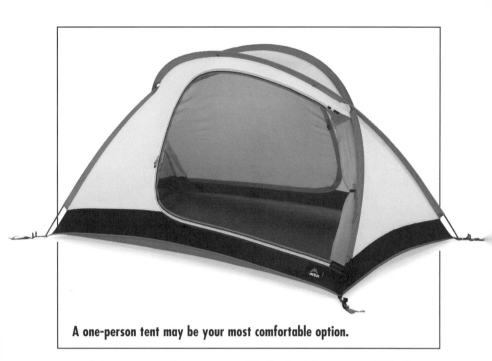

A one-person tent may be your most comfortable option.

enough to accommodate your gear? Is the tent long enough? Is the tent constructed from materials that are appropriate for the types of trips you're most likely to take? For example, if you'll be doing most of your trekking in the desert, consider a tent with lots of mesh and good ventilation. If cold climes are more to your liking, make sure mesh "windows" can be zipped shut to keep the heat from escaping.

But what good is a superlight, high-tech tent if you can't set it up by yourself? Some tents require the help of a second person during setup; the only way to find out is to put up the tent in the store before you put down your credit card. Can you pitch the tent easily by yourself? What if it was raining? Windy? How easily does the rainfly fasten to the tent? Could you do it in the middle of the night—by yourself?

Once you've found the tent that's right for you, it's always a good idea to reinforce the material's water-repellent properties. Purchase a tube of seam sealer and apply it to all the seams on the tent. Also consider using a ground cloth to keep the living space dry during storms and to keep the tent floor from getting ripped or punctured. Before you settle in for the evening, make sure the ground cloth isn't sticking out from under the tent. If it is, rain will roll off the rainfly onto the ground cloth and create a pool of water under the tent. To prevent this, use a ground cloth that is smaller than the floor of the tent.

A slightly smaller, lighter alternative to a tent—and one that

Lightweight and easy to set up, a bivy is preferred by many soloists.

For the minimalist, a tarp is the way to go.

requires minimal setup—is a bivouac bag, or bivy sac. These durable, waterproof shells slip around your sleeping bag and have become the preferred shelter for many soloists. The drawback to the bivy, however, is that it confines you to a very small space. If the weather is inclement or mosquitoes are in hot pursuit, you'll be a mummified camper in a bivy. Some models provide a mesh-lined space around your head that allows you to sit up and read or write and still stay protected from the elements. But it's quite a challenge to wait out a long storm in a bivy!

The tarp is your third alternative and the one that is preferred by the minimalist. Tarps are inexpensive, weigh very little, and take up minimal space in your pack. If you select the tarp as your shelter of choice, think about how you will set it up. Some hikers like to string the tarp between trees. Others drape the tarp over a hiking stick to create a tepeelike structure. Hiking sticks and trekking poles can also be used to create a high end so that water will easily run off the tarp. Some hikers drape the tarp over a cord strung between two trees, then stake the sides of the tarp into the ground. Rigging a tarp to protect you from the elements is not as easy as it may look; the setup strategy requires a little more forethought for a tarp than it does for a tent or a bivy sac. Be aware also that tarps provide no protection from biting insects, nor do they provide the warmth of a tent or bivy.

For a Sound Sleep

For me, one of the most enjoyable aspects of camping solo comes in the evening when I organize my belongings in the tent just the way I like them—flashlight and watch in the tent pocket, water bottle by my head, journal and pen beside my makeshift pillow (usually a fleece jacket)—and I settle into a luxuriously soft bed: a full-length inflatable sleeping mattress beneath a cozy goose-down sleeping bag. I don't have to worry about disturbing a tentmate with my reading light or a trip to the bathroom in the middle of the night, and I can take up as much space as I like! But these evenings are only as enjoyable as my sleeping bag and mattress are comfortable. Since you won't be able to inch your way onto your partner's superior sleeping mattress in the middle of the night or use your partner's body heat if your sleeping bag isn't warm enough, it becomes a matter of safety as well as comfort that you choose appropriate sleeping gear for your trip.

Sleeping Bags

For decades gear aficionados have debated the benefits of down versus synthetic sleeping bags. Down bags tend to pack smaller, weigh less, and cost more than their synthetic counterparts. While their

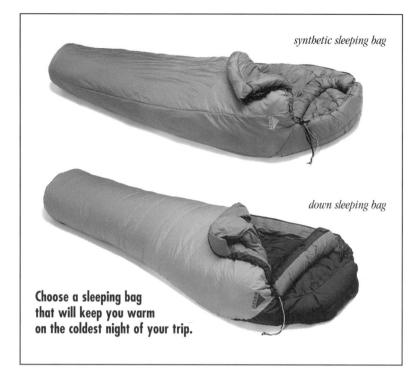

synthetic sleeping bag

down sleeping bag

Choose a sleeping bag that will keep you warm on the coldest night of your trip.

warmth now rivals that of down bags, synthetic bags tend to be bulkier but less expensive. Some people maintain that a synthetic fill retains more warmth than down if the bag gets wet. The choice, of course, is up to you.

Whichever fill material you choose, make certain your bag has a temperature rating lower than the lowest temperature you expect to encounter. Since it is entirely up to you to generate enough heat to stay warm, choose a bag that is fully functional and appropriate for your trip.

If you are shorter than 5 feet, 5 inches, consider buying a short sleeping bag. A smaller bag will save room in your pack and keep you warmer at night, since you won't have to heat all the extra space at your feet.

Also look for other features: A drawcord around the hood allows you to cinch the hood around your head on very cold nights. A two-way zipper is a nice feature on warm evenings; it allows you to unzip the bag from the bottom, making it possible to air out your feet.

Your bag will perform better and last longer if you store it in a durable waterproof stuff sack while you're in the backcountry. Each morning, unzip the bag and let it dry completely before packing it up.

At home, store the bag in a large cotton storage sack or lay it on a shelf in your closet. This helps maintain the fill material's loft, which means that the bag will keep you warmer for longer.

Sleeping Mattresses

While a comfortable night's sleep is certainly important, so is the size and weight of your backpack. Remember, if every item you bring is the biggest, burliest piece of equipment created, you'll end up wobbling down the trail with gear stacked over your head like a pile of pancakes. I value a soft bed and was willing to spend more money on an inflatable sleeping mattress. It is long but narrow, extremely comfortable, lightweight, and packs into a tiny stuff sack. For those who favor an inflatable pad, there are numerous models to choose from. They all generally provide more comfort than their foam-pad counterparts, but, as you can imagine, they are more expensive. Foam pads are inexpensive, light, bulky, and virtually indestructible. I also know a soloist or two who choose to forgo the sleeping mattress altogether and are content with sleeping on their extra clothes. What trade-offs and sacrifices are *you* willing to make?

After testing a few sleeping mattresses in the store, ask yourself the following questions: Is the pad long enough? Is it comfortable? Are the size and weight acceptable? How small is it when it's rolled up? Do you desire a pad that converts into a camp chair? Whether you decide on a very large pad or a tiny one, a mattress of some sort not only makes

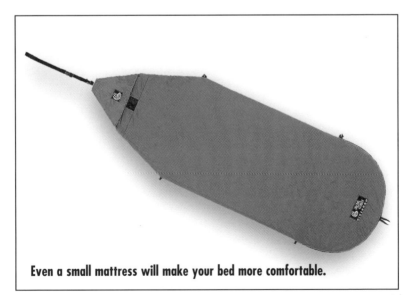

Even a small mattress will make your bed more comfortable.

solo travel more comfortable, but it also provides insulation between you and the cold ground and can add considerable warmth to your night in the woods.

Hiker's Wardrobe

One day, while picking my way through Maine's North Woods, I ran into a woman whose mismatched outfit caught my attention. The collar of a bright orange and green Hawaiian print long-underwear shirt stuck out from beneath a yellow and purple striped windbreaker. To keep the mosquitoes at bay, she had wrapped a blue and pink scarf around her head, babushka style. Fraying khaki shorts were held together with multicolored patches, and she had pulled up her electric blue knee-high socks as far as they'd go. After talking with her it became clear she wasn't trying to make a statement or attract attention (heck! who would she by trying to impress in the woods anyway?). These were simply the items that were practical to bring on this particular trip. Too bad if they weren't color coordinated. The lesson here is function before fashion.

Clothing

Unless you'll be hiking in extremely hot, arid regions (in which case, the goal is to stay cool and covered with light, breathable materials like cotton), the key to clothing selection is to choose items that will keep you warm and dry. As a safety precaution for the soloist, it's best to prepare for temperatures lower than you'd expect to encounter. Think in layers, starting with a light base layer and working your way out to a windproof or waterproof shell. Unless you're in an extremely hot area, all items should be made from silk, wool, or synthetic materials like fleece or polypropylene. These materials wick moisture away from your skin and dry quickly, which will keep you warmer and more comfortable than cotton. On most trips the only cotton item I bring is a T-shirt that serves as my clean sleeping shirt for a truly cozy evening.

The wardrobe I bring on a backpacking trip is almost identical to what I bring on a dayhike. Women can begin the layering system with a synthetic sports bra. I prefer one with lots of mesh for ventilation. In any climate, I carry a long-sleeve long underwear base layer, a thick fleece jacket, and a waterproof shell. If it's warm I wear a synthetic tank top. Whether I'll be hiking for three days or three hours, I always bring a hat and gloves; I can't tell you how many times that little hat has made all the difference in my staying comfortable.

The same philosophy applies to the bottom half. You have a myriad of options for quick-drying shorts and hiking pants that allow plenty of

Layer up in cold weather with long underwear, fleece, and a waterproof jacket.

In warm weather you'll be comfortable wearing loose, quick-drying shorts and a silk or synthetic shirt.

room for full range of motion, whether you're hopping across rocks or cruising on the flats. Many hiking pants have zippers midthigh so that you can convert the pants to shorts. In addition to the shorts or pants I hike in, I also carry waterproof pants to wear in the rain or around camp on cool evenings. Depending on where you're going, it may also be prudent to carry long underwear for your bottom half. Whatever you do, stay away from jeans, belts, and cotton pants.

Though it may sound excessive, your wardrobe for a day trip may be quite similar. I always carry a hat, fleece jacket, and waterproof jacket and begin my hike believing that even if I'm welcomed into the woods with a crystal-clear sky, sometime during the day it will rain. More than once I've set out on an afternoon jaunt in shorts and a tank top and returned in hat, gloves, and full rain suit!

Footwear

Anyone who has hiked with wet, cold, or blistered feet can attest to how important proper footwear is. A problem with your feet— whether it's from a kink in the inner lining of your boot, from wearing cotton socks, or from wearing waterlogged boots—is likely to cut your trip short or overshadow good moments with memories of pain and discomfort. To make sure your feet stay in top shape, spend some time putting together an appropriate footwear package.

SOCKS

Start by selecting wool or synthetic hiking socks and a silk or synthetic liner sock. Two socks will slide against each other when you walk, creating friction between your socks instead of against your skin. Always bring an extra pair of socks; nothing is worse than cold feet and no dry socks to warm them up. In the morning I often change into socks I wore the previous day (even if they're still a little damp and smelly) so that one pair always stays clean and dry. Some hikers even bring an extra pair on day trips and change into the fresh ones for the final strides back to the car.

BOOTS

Boots are a critical component to the footwear package, so spend some time finding boots that are appropriate for the trips you're most likely to take. You'll be just as uncomfortable walking on a glacier in running shoes as you will backpacking the Dakota grasslands with mountaineering boots. Don't get beefy boots just because you *might* take that trip up to Rocky Rubble Rest but all your other hikes will be on gentle to moderate trails. I opt for the lightest, most comfortable boot I can find that still provides ample support on rocky terrain. Often, especially on dayhikes on gentle terrain, a running shoe works just fine. Otherwise a lightweight hiking boot should suffice for even moderately technical day trips. Unless my pack is very heavy or the terrain very rocky, I use my lightweight dayhiking boots for most backpacking trips as well.

Spend sufficient time to get boots that fit. Ask to talk with the boot expert at your local outfitting store. It's a waste of time to get fitted for boots by someone who isn't familiar with the nuances of footwear for hikers. Try on as many different brands and models as you can stand; this is the only way you'll be able to find what a truly comfortable fit feels like. The tongue of the boot should lie comfortably across the top of your foot, you should be able to wriggle your toes, and the heel should feel snug. Walk around the store for twenty minutes to see if any uncomfortable spots develop.

Your footwear package should consist of wool or synthetic socks, sturdy hiking boots, and gaiters.

Consider a good boot a measure of prevention against blisters, twisted ankles, and hypothermia. As a soloist, preventing such problems is critical—hobbling out of the backcountry unassisted is no fun at all.

Your quest for proper footwear doesn't end with the purchase, however. Proper care for your investment will significantly increase the life and function of the boot. I once worked as a backcountry ranger in Alaska. My job involved fording rivers and bushwhacking through dense brush for four months. To keep my boots from disintegrating and to keep the leather from cracking during the constant cycle of soaking and drying, I brushed them with a water-repellency treatment once a week. You can find a variety of treatments at your local outfitting store, and a salesperson can help you determine which treatment is appropriate for the type of boot you have.

As exciting as it is to get new boots, don't rush off on a long hike without first breaking them in. The break-in process involves spending incrementally more time in your boots until it is comfortable to wear them all day long. In some cases it may take months before they are ready for multiple-day excursions.

GAITERS

You may also want to add a pair of gaiters to your footwear package. Gaiters wrap around your ankle and shin to prevent debris or snow (depending on where you are) from getting inside your boot. Full-length gaiters are also helpful on cross-country trips; they keep your lower legs from getting scratched by unfriendly brush. Shorter ankle-gaiters are nice on warm-weather trips, especially if you have a tendency to kick sand or small rocks into your boots.

Kitchen

The dayhiker's kitchen is fairly simple; you need only be concerned with food and water. I usually pack plenty of snacks and bring more water than I think I'll drink. Since you can fill your water bottles at home, you probably don't need to worry about treating water on your hike. Still, I always keep a few iodine tablets in my daypack for emergencies, in case I spill my water.

The backpacker's kitchen requires a little more strategizing. In addition to food you'll need a water purification device, a stove, fuel, and cookware.

Food

On backpacking trips it's smart to bring a little extra food in case you end up staying out longer than you planned: In an emergency it may

Ending the day with a hot meal is one of hiking's sweet rewards.

take longer for rescue crews to find you if you're traveling by yourself. A balanced diet of healthful, high-calorie foods provides the energy necessary for extended physical exertion and plays a big role in keeping you warm. Dried meats, nuts, pasta, rice, dried fruits and vegetables, cereal, and powdered drink mixes are all good options. If you're used to planning trips with others, you'll find that preparing a menu for yourself is much easier than taking into account an entire

A: Safely store your food by attaching your food bag to the end of a length of rope or cord. Toss the bag over a branch that is at least 15 feet high and make sure the bag is at least 5 feet from the tree trunk.

B: Tie a second bag (weighted with toiletries, cookware, etc.) as high as you can on the other end of the rope, then use a long stick to push the lower bag up higher. **C:** In the morning, use the stick to retrieve your bags.

group's dietary preferences and determining the right quantities of food. I usually take the same amount of food I normally eat in a day, plus a plethora of snacks. Just be careful that your snacks don't precipitate a sugar binge; choose high-energy snacks that consist of something more than chocolate-coated sugar puffs. A hiker fueled on satisfying, nutritious meals is more likely to stay energized and comfortable and less likely to fatigue or get injured. Consider your diet a measure of prevention against injury and illness.

In addition to nutrition, you'll want to pay attention to how much food items weigh and how easy they are to pack. Since you're responsible for carrying all the equipment, you have enough to worry about without adding heavy or bulky food items to your pack. You can probably imagine that foods like canned soup, soda, and rice cakes are not the best options. Choose foods that won't spoil, and that pack calories and nutrients into a small space. Consider foods like nuts, seeds, hard-boiled eggs, beans, cheese, peanut butter, pepperoni, and energy bars. In many cases your backcountry menu may be quite similar to what you eat at home.

In many parts of the country, wildlife may find your food as appealing as you do, so you'll need to be clever and careful with foodstuffs, especially before you turn in for the night. Critters like mice, porcupines, deer, skunks, and bears are likely to be attracted to your food, or to items like toothpaste and sunscreen that may smell like food to many animals. To ensure that the food you brought ends up in the right belly, it is often a good idea to hang your food in a tree. Tie a length of cord to your food bag, and hoist the bag over a sturdy tree limb that's about 15 feet off the ground. Tie a second bag of equal weight (I usually fill this one with toiletries and cookware) to the other end of the cord. Use a stick to push the bags up as high as they'll go. In the morning, use the stick to retrieve the bags.

This is just one of many food storage techniques. Check with local land management officials (at a visitor center or ranger station) to learn which techniques work best in the area you'll be hiking. Some camp-grounds may have bear poles or food lockers for you to use.

Water

Since viruses, bacteria, parasites, and organic chemicals can be found just about everywhere, you'll need to treat water before you drink it. There are three ways to do this: boiling, filtering, and using a chemical treatment.

Whichever method you prefer, make a point to stop often to replenish your water supply. In an emergency it's more important to drink from a questionable source than not drink at all. Many people prefer to store water in a wide-mouthed water bottle, which can be stowed in a pouch on the side of the pack. These bottles, typically made of a durable material called Lexan, won't leak or retain odors like average plastic bottles or cyclists' water bottles. Other hikers prefer backpacks with a built-in hydration system. Water is stored in a bag inside the pack and flows through a tube and mouthpiece, which can be clipped to the pack's shoulder strap for easy access. Never before has it been so easy to stay hydrated!

A water filter helps make water taste good.

BOILING

Boiling water kills everything in it, which makes this method quite safe; however, you can imagine the inconvenience of setting up the stove every few hours and waiting for your water to cool before you drink it. The hassle of boiling water has made the other two methods very popular.

FILTERING

Just as there is a wide range of models, weights, and prices to consider when purchasing a water filter, there is also a wide range of filtering capabilities. Learn the differences between water filters from your local outfitter, as some filters (called purifiers) include a chemical treatment that gets rid of viruses, heavy metals, herbicides, and pesticides. Filtered water generally tastes good, and, unlike the two other methods, you can drink the water right away.

CHEMICAL TREATMENT

A chemical treatment like iodine tablets works well because it's simple, inexpensive, and lightweight, but iodine takes at least twenty minutes to kill the microorganisms and many hikers turn up their noses at the taste of chemically treated water unless they're on the brink of dehydration. Iodine kills pretty much everything except a little protozoan called *Cryptosporidium*. I prefer iodine on short trips and take a water purifier on longer ones. Keep in mind that iodine may be harmful if you're pregnant or have thyroid problems.

Stove, Fuel, Cookware

Since maintaining a low pack weight is a top priority for many soloists, I've noticed that a fair number of hikers cut weight by leaving behind the stove, fuel, and cookware. This is certainly a legitimate strategy, especially if you'll be backpacking for only a day or two. A variety of cold foods and snacks can sustain a person for quite a while, and many minimalists aren't inconvenienced in the least to go without a hot meal.

To many others, however, preparing a hot evening meal is a coveted ritual. The purr of a stove and the hiss of boiling water gives hikers peace of mind in cold conditions. They know that if they get into trouble, they at least have the ability to make a cup of tea or a hot meal to reinvigorate their system. For those of us who prefer to cook our backcountry meals, the single-burner camp stove is the way to go. They are compact, lightweight, and can boil water in a matter of minutes. Whether you opt for a stove that burns liquid fuel like white gas (often referred to as Coleman fuel) or a stove that burns propane/butane canisters, make sure you know how to operate the stove by yourself. Practice lighting it a few times at home before you venture into the backcountry. The more familiar you are with your equipment, the easier time you'll have if something should break. If you don't know how to clean the fuel line and perform basic maintenance on your stove, ask a salesperson or a knowledgeable friend to show you. If you're carrying liquid fuel, prevent a disastrous leak on the trail by storing fuel in an outside pocket or somewhere where a leak is not likely to lead to fuel-soaked food and clothing.

A soloist's cookware should be kept to a minimum and may include a single-burner camp stove.

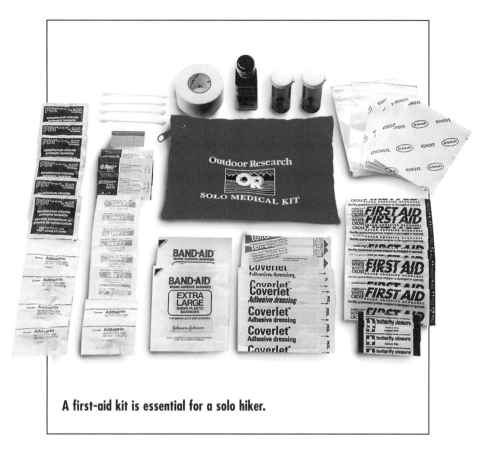

A first-aid kit is essential for a solo hiker.

As a soloist it is easy to keep cookware to a minimum. One pot and one spoon is typically all you'll need. I also bring a small mug for hot drinks and a pot gripper to handle hot cookware.

Odds and Ends

Your packing job would not be complete without adding a few additional items to your growing pile of gear. Fortunately, these items tend to be quite small and weigh very little.

On every dayhike or backpacking trip, you'll want to carry a first-aid kit. Make sure your kit contains the following items:

◆ *first-aid booklet*

◆ *elastic bandage*

◆ *sterile gauze dressings*

Solo Hiking

Your first-aid kit should include a knife, a headlamp, and a hygiene kit, which may include a toothbrush, toothpaste, lip balm, sunscreen, and a small brush.

- *roller bandage*
- *triangular bandage*
- *antibiotic ointment*
- *ten-cubic-centimeter irrigation syringe with eighteen-gauge catheter tip for flushing wounds*
- *dressing for blisters*
- *non-aspirin pain reliever*
- *Band-Aids*

A small knife is another good addition to every hiker's pack. It can be used to cut materials from a first-aid kit, is handy to cut cord or tape for a quick gear repair, and is useful in the kitchen when you need to cut food or packaging. You'll find that a very small blade will service most backcountry needs.

You'll want to carry a small flashlight or headlamp on overnight trips. Not only will it come in handy if you like to end your day reading or writing, but a light is also invaluable during an unplanned night hike or when you need to secure the rainfly in the middle of the night.

The final item that ought to come with you on any backpacking trip is a hygiene kit. I take a small tube of toothpaste, toothbrush, small comb, hair tie, lip balm, and sunscreen. These items fit nicely into a small, resealable plastic bag. What may be most significant about the hygiene kit are the items not included: Trust me, you won't regret leaving soap, shampoo, deodorant, and perfume behind.

Packs

You are now ready to select a pack in which you'll tote all your carefully selected gear. The two most important things the solo hiker must look for when selecting a backpack are (1) a pack with a large enough capacity to tote all your gear; and (2) a comfortable fit.

If you're used to hiking with others, the amount of room you'll need for a solo trip may surprise you. When hiking with a partner, one person may carry the stove while the other person takes the fuel. You might opt for the tent poles and ground cloth while your partner takes the tent body and rainfly. Usually only one water filter, first-aid kit, and cookset is needed per group. When you go solo, you're responsible for carrying everything, which can quickly fill a pack and make the load a bit heavier than you're used to.

It is worth noting that pack size is different from pack volume.

backpack with internal frame, designed for three to four days

daypack

backpack with internal frame, designed for seven to ten days

backpack with external frame, designed for five to seven days

Select a comfortable backpack that is large enough to accommodate all your gear.

A pack might come in three sizes (small, medium, and large), which correspond to the length of your torso. Pack volume, which can be anything from 2,000 to 9,000 cubic inches, defines the amount of space in the packbag. This means that if you have a very long torso and plan on carrying a light load, you can choose a large-size pack with a small volume. To find a backpack with an appropriate volume, pack different backpacks with all the equipment (including clothes and food) you'll be carrying on your trip. You'll eventually find one that accommodates your gear without much room left over.

Now, the second consideration: You must find a pack that can support the weight of the full load and still maintain a comfortable fit. When testing the comfort quotient of different packs, understand that we're aiming for a comfortable fit with a *loaded* backpack. Even a pack without a hip belt feels comfortable when it's empty!

What about the long-standing debate over internal- versus external-frame backpacks? Proponents of internal-frame packs (which have a frame inside the packbag) claim that these packs may be more appropriate for rugged, uneven terrain since they sit closer to your back. Others claim that external-frame packs (which have a packbag mounted to the outside of a rigid frame) are more comfortable when walking on gentle terrain. In my opinion, it doesn't matter which type you get. Listen to your body, not to the gear magazines or to your overly enthusiastic cousin who swears that her pack is the end-all be-all of packs. If the fully loaded pack still feels comfortable after walking through the store for thirty minutes, you've probably found the right pack.

Don't be fooled by extra straps and gadgets; they will be helpful to you only if they are straps and gadgets that you need. Ice ax loops are useful only if you'll be carrying an ice ax. Respect your quirky habits and personal preferences: Some folks like many little pockets while others prefer one large compartment. Do you prefer an external pocket for a water bottle or a pack with a built-in hydration system? The choice is yours.

Packing the Pack

How you arrange your belongings in the pack depends on the design of your pack and on your personal preferences. Most hikers squeeze the sleeping bag into the bottom of the pack and pile heavier items closer to their back. Your arrangement will likely depend on your pack, which usually will have many small pockets or one large compartment. You may find it easier to strap bulky items like a tent or sleeping mattress to the outside of the pack. Whatever strategy you employ, it is

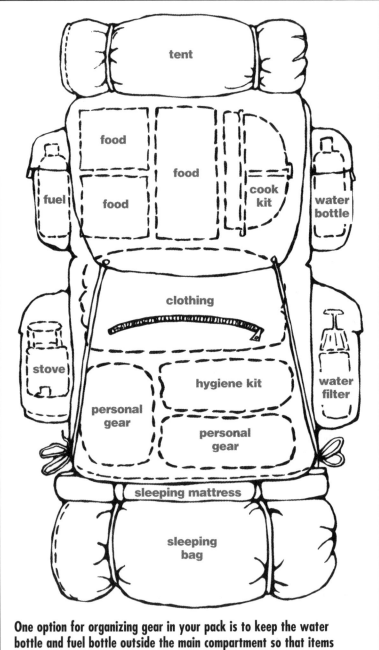

tent

food

food

fuel

food

cook kit

water bottle

clothing

stove

hygiene kit

personal gear

personal gear

water filter

sleeping mattress

sleeping bag

One option for organizing gear in your pack is to keep the water bottle and fuel bottle outside the main compartment so that items such as the first-aid kit and rain jacket are easy to get in.

imperative to store such items as a rain jacket and first-aid kit in easy-to-reach places like an outside pocket or top pouch. Especially when you're traveling alone, it may be important to have such items readily available in an emergency.

Putting the Pack on Your Back

Before you try on a pack, loosen all the straps. Bend your knees and lift the pack onto your thigh. Put one arm through a shoulder strap, then swing the pack onto your shoulder. Slip the other arm through the other shoulder strap as if you're putting on a jacket. Now cinch the hip belt snugly around your hips. The belt should not be cinched around your waist where it constricts your breathing and puts pressure on sensitive internal organs, nor should it be so low that it interferes with your stride. The weight of the pack should rest where your body can most easily support it: on your skeleton. Now tighten the shoulder straps, adjust the load-lifter straps by your ears, and clasp the sternum strap across your chest.

Every now and then I see a solo hiker lumbering down the trail with stacks of gear teetering above his or her head and rolls of gear lashed to the sides of the pack, the whole contraption swaying with every step. These persons are intent on bringing everything they can possibly carry into the backcountry. If you have the ability to support that kind of weight, there's nothing wrong with that style of travel, but when you're by yourself, you may actually need assistance putting the pack on.

Whether you're a proponent of the Gigantic Pack school or would simply like to be easier on your body, here's a strategy that will allow you to put on the pack without straining your back. With bent knees, carefully lift your pack and place it on something about 3 feet high, such as a tree stump, picnic table, or large rock. Turn your back to the pack and slip your arms through the shoulder straps. Bend your knees, lean slightly forward, and gently shift the weight of the pack from the other surface to your shoulders. Tighten the hip belt and the other straps, and off you go.

Just because you're a solo hiker and responsible for all the gear doesn't mean that your pack has to tip the scales. Many solo hikers are minimalists, determined to travel light despite not having the luxury of sharing gear. To learn more about ultralight gear and hiking styles, search the Internet for "ultralight hiking" and you'll find tips from folks whose packs never weigh more than twelve pounds! If you pay attention to the weight of every item and consider going without the double frappacino maker and the portable CD player, you can maintain a reasonable pack weight.

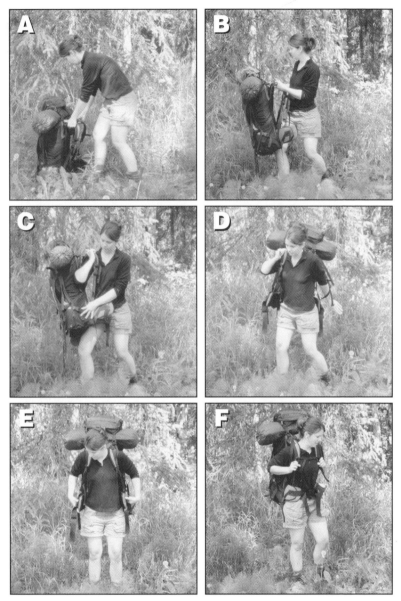

There are six steps for putting on the backpack. **A:** First, face the backpack and take hold of the shoulder straps. **B:** With bent knees, lift the pack to your thigh. **C:** Slip one arm through the shoulder strap. **D:** Swing the pack onto your back and slide the other arm through the other shoulder strap. **E:** Clasp and tighten the hip belt. **F:** Make sure the shoulder straps are taut, clasp the sternum strap across your chest, and you're ready to go!

Here's another technique for putting on a backpack, especially a heavy one.
A: With knees bent, lift the pack onto a tree stump or a picnic table. **B:** Turn around and put your arms through the shoulder straps as if you're putting on a jacket. With knees bent, lean forward to shift the weight of the pack from the tree stump to your back, then slowly straighten up and secure the straps.

Equipment Checklist

The following checklists are not exhaustive; many hikers require gear to meet special needs (contact lenses or medications, for example). I know one hiker who won't leave home without a certain stuffed animal; it serves as a good-luck charm. Conversely, don't feel obligated to take every listed item; choose gear that's practical for your particular outing. Deciding to bring items like a journal or binoculars is a matter of personal preference and only you can determine if the weight and space of the item is worth it. Bring the item if it will significantly enhance your experience or if it serves as a safety precaution (like insect repellent or cord to hang food away from bears).

DAYHIKER'S CHECKLIST

- ❑ daypack
- ❑ appropriate clothes
  (including hat and rain jacket)
- ❑ water
- ❑ snacks
- ❑ map
- ❑ compass
- ❑ iodine tablets
- ❑ first-aid kit
  (contents listed in chapter 1)
- ❑ lightweight hiking boots
  or running shoes
- ❑ gaiters
- ❑ sunscreen
- ❑ lip balm
- ❑ sunglasses
- ❑ camera
- ❑ journal and writing implement
- ❑ sketch book
- ❑ binoculars
- ❑ hand lens
- ❑ field guides

BACKPACKER'S CHECKLIST

- ❑ backpack with fly or
  lined with large garbage bag
- ❑ tent, bivy, or tarp
- ❑ sleeping bag
- ❑ sleeping mattress
- ❑ map and compass
- ❑ water bottles or hydration system
- ❑ light
- ❑ knife
- ❑ first-aid kit
  (contents listed in chapter 1)
- ❑ mesh head net
- ❑ trekking poles
- ❑ watch
- ❑ camera
- ❑ guidebook
- ❑ journal and writing implement
- ❑ pepper spray
- ❑ parachute cord
- ❑ trowel
- ❑ umbrella

- ❏ repair kit (patches, ripstop nylon tape, thread and needle, safety pins)
- ❏ binoculars
- ❏ hiking boots
- ❏ gaiters
- ❏ hiking socks and liner socks
- ❏ camp shoes (sandals or sneakers)
- ❏ underwear
- ❏ long underwear
- ❏ shorts, hiking pants
- ❏ hiking shirt
- ❏ sleeping shirt
- ❏ rain gear (jacket and pants)
- ❏ hat
- ❏ gloves
- ❏ bandanna
- ❏ water purification system
- ❏ stove and lighter
- ❏ mug
- ❏ pot with lid
- ❏ pot gripper
- ❏ spoon
- ❏ sponge
- ❏ food
- ❏ toothbrush and toothpaste
- ❏ comb
- ❏ sunscreen
- ❏ lip balm
- ❏ toilet paper and resealable plastic bag for used toilet paper
- ❏ sunglasses
- ❏ sunhat
- ❏ bug repellent

FOR WOMEN

- ❏ tampons, pads, moist wipes, extra resealable plastic bags

MT. LEBANON PUBLIC LIBRARY

Safety Concerns *for the* Solo Traveler

Since we'll spend a fair amount of time dealing with safety issues for the soloist, let's first take a minute to consider that solo travel can actually be safer than traveling with a group. In a group, individual accountability tends to decrease as group size increases. Equipment is shared and you rely on others for safety and comfort. But what if Dan decided to lighten his pack at the last minute and left the group's first-aid kit in the car? Decisions made by a group can often be rash and ill-informed. Group members can convince one another that the tricky route actually doesn't look so bad. Or one overbearing group member can pressure the others into attempting more miles than they're capable of hiking. When you're on your own, you can make responsible decisions and not feel pressured to accept a poor plan just because the majority appears to favor it. Other people's poor judgment won't affect you.

Many people, however, perceive solo trips as more dangerous simply because if something should happen—a twisted ankle, a snakebite, a wrong turn—it may take a long time for someone to find you and help you out. In the critical moments of a medical emergency, it doesn't take long for an injured hiker to go from bad to worse.

Rather than sit at home in order to eliminate the risk entirely, you can learn certain skills and use good judgment to prevent or avoid unfavorable situations, and you can learn how to best deal with difficult situations should they arise. Prevention starts before you hit the trail—it begins when you plan your trip.

Planning

Territory, Time, and Terrain

It should come as no surprise that a novice hiker is likely to get into trouble if he or she plans a two-week trip in Wyoming's rugged Wind River Range, hopes to travel 18 miles every day, and has never been to Wyoming. "But I want to challenge myself," you say! There are many ways to challenge yourself in the backcountry without embarking on a high-risk mission. Most people will find enough surprises, risks, and challenges on a route that is well within their ability level. Somehow, just being out there, dealing with unpredictable weather and trail conditions and adjusting to solitude and open space, is enough to satisfy even the most adventurous souls.

Consider what you have to gain by undertaking a certain challenge, and decide if you can be comfortable with the risks involved. The key is to choose a place that offers a hiking experience that will match your ability level. Especially on your first solo outing, I recommend selecting a destination that you are at least somewhat familiar with. If something should go wrong during a trip in familiar territory, you will feel more confident finding the fastest way out.

Think about how much time you have and how long you'd like to be out there. You may find you're comfortable hiking no more than three hours by yourself. If this is the case, plan a dayhike that can be completed easily within your time frame. If you're up for a multiday trip, start out small with an overnight trip. Use your first trips as tests to make sure your gear is fully functional and to get used to the feeling of hiking and camping on your own. Again, work within your ability level.

Consider the terrain. Select a route you'll be comfortable hiking. For example, if you're afraid of heights, avoid the route that traverses the edge of a steep canyon wall. Also consider that you'll travel much farther on a flat, smooth trail than you will hopping across a boulder field or negotiating a steep scree slope. Study a map of the area and talk with people who have been there to determine what type of terrain you'll encounter.

The season can also affect trail conditions. For example, a trip to the desert Southwest may be much more enjoyable if you avoid the height of summer. If you walk through a high-mountain region in early spring, expect to encounter deep snow and avalanche conditions.

Give careful consideration to trip planning. It's a good idea to consult maps, guidebooks, and other people who have been there.

After a few successful day trips, consider an overnight foray. Once you feel comfortable navigating by yourself and using all your equipment, you are ready for multiple-day backpacking trips. Again it is best to plan reasonable mileage and stick to low-risk terrain. If you desire to travel cross-country—that is, leave the trail system and create your own route—know that this is a risky undertaking. Compared with searching main trails, it is much more difficult for rescue teams to find a lost hiker if they have to search trail-less areas.

If you're not exactly sure where to go, start with a trip to the local chamber of commerce or visitor center. The folks staffing these centers ought to be familiar with public lands in the area and know whom to contact for more information. Visit your local outfitting store; employees should have firsthand knowledge of local trails and trail conditions. Guidebooks are a good source of information, as are ranger stations and public lands offices. Find the nearest state or national park, Forest

Service or BLM lands, or national wildlife refuge. Local hiking clubs and conservation organizations can often make excellent recommendations. Or purchase a topographic map from a local map store or outfitter or from the Earth Science Information Center (see address below), which compiles information from numerous sources to develop maps of public lands, and come up with a plan of your own.

ESIC Headquarters
U.S. Geological Survey
12201 Sunrise Valley Drive
Reston, VA 20192
(888) 275-8747
mapping.usgs.gov/

No matter where you decide to go, the most important thing you can do is leave an itinerary with friends or family and drop one off at the nearest visitor center or ranger station. Include a description of the route you plan to take, where you expect to camp each night, and what day you plan to return. The color of your tent, any medical conditions you may have, and your license plate number if you're parking at a trailhead are good things to add to your itinerary, as they may expedite the rescue process. If you get into trouble and don't come out when

Before you depart, review your itinerary with a ranger.

expected, you'll know that someone back home will initiate a search and at least have a general idea of where to find you. Even for a short dayhike, it is always best to tell someone where you're going. My family has gotten in the habit of leaving a note on the kitchen table to let everyone else know what time they left, where they went, and when they expect to be back.

Safety Precaution or False Sense of Security?

Hikers often carry with them into the woods a fear for their safety. Sometimes they are afraid because they're traveling in unfamiliar territory and don't know what type of weather, wildlife, or terrain may lie ahead. Sometimes they're afraid of other people.

When you head into the wilderness, and especially when you go alone, it is important to feel that you'd be able to protect yourself in the unlikely event of an attack. It is in the planning stages that you must decide what, if any, form of personal protection you will take. So let's take a moment to talk about three things people often take into the backcountry to help them feel safer.

DOGS

Many hikers prefer to travel with a canine companion, believing their dog will sense danger in people with bad intentions and will ward off an aggressor. People also like to think their dog will fend off aggressive wildlife or will at least provide a distraction while their owner gets away. The reality is that dogs can indeed provide some security, but it really depends on the dog—and on the situation. In most cases I believe dogs provide a *sense* of security more than they serve as reliable protectors. They are excellent companions and can make a good trip even more enjoyable, but they probably can't offer much protection against an attack by a grizzly bear or a person with a gun.

Also recognize that dogs are a big responsibility. It is up to you to make sure your pet is safe and healthy and is not disrupting others. If you do bring a dog, for protection or for companionship, be a responsible owner by obeying leash laws and making sure your pet is not annoying other hikers or harassing wildlife. A backcountry dog ought to be under strict voice control at all times.

GUNS

When people ask me if I carry a gun on backcountry outings, I reply with an emphatic "No!" While some areas, like parts of Alaska, may warrant carrying a gun for protection against wildlife, I believe that for 99 percent of backcountry travel, carrying a gun is more of a threat to you and to the people around you than it is a safety precaution.

Make sure your K-9 companion is leashed and under voice control at all times.

Indeed, tragic events have occurred in the backcountry. But such events are rare and in most cases were surprise attacks that could not have been prevented, even if the victim had been armed with a gun. Unless you are on a hunting trip, please leave the gun behind. Be aware, too, that it is illegal to carry firearms on many public lands, including national parks.

Recognize that you're probably already carrying a weapon: Consider your trekking poles, pepper spray, or pocket knife all the artillery you'll ever need. You may also want to take a self-defense class. If you're armed with a few basic skills and common sense, you'll probably rest easier than if you pack a .44 on your hip.

If you choose to carry a cell phone, respect other hikers by stepping off the trail and making calls when no one else is around.

CELL PHONES

As communications technology continues to grow, cell phones are finding their way into an increasing number of backpacks. Calling phones their lifeline to civilization, many hikers are reluctant to hit the trail without one. Some soloists feel much safer with a phone, believing that in an emergency a phone will greatly expedite the rescue process. In some instances phones have played a role in helping hikers return safely, and they certainly make people *feel* safer, but cell phones can also be unreliable and give people a false sense of security. If you decide to try a more difficult route or stay out longer than usual because you think, *I can always call if I get into trouble,* you may be putting yourself in a very dangerous situation. Your cell phone may not work, especially in the mountains and in remote areas. Also, not all emergencies can be solved with a phone; many medical emergencies may require immediate attention. Even if rescuers are notified quickly, weather conditions or technical terrain may prevent a speedy rescue.

There's also been a growing concern about hikers calling for help when they're simply tired and hungry and not when their lives are in

BASIC ESSENTIALS

any real danger. Very expensive and risky searches have been initiated for hikers with only minor discomforts. If you do bring a phone, please use it only in real emergencies.

Also keep in mind that many hikers view such technology as an intrusion into their wilderness experience. If you do elect to bring a phone, show your respect for other recreationists by keeping it off when it's in your pack and using it only when others aren't around.

Skills

More important than bringing a dog or cell phone to make you feel safer is equipping yourself with the knowledge to prevent or avoid dangerous situations in the first place. In this section we'll talk about essential skills for the soloist: map and compass skills, route finding, and river crossings.

Map and Compass

The best prevention against getting lost is bringing a map and knowing how to read it. Especially on dayhikes, it can be tempting to take off without a map or to use the trail description pamphlet that you picked up at the visitor center. Be wary of these: They give you a general overview of the area but don't show enough detail for you to navigate by. No matter where you're headed, invest in a topographic map. These are detailed maps that show major features like lakes, rivers, trails, roads,

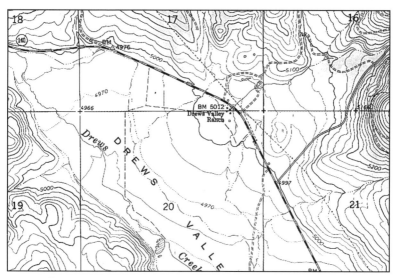

Topographic map.

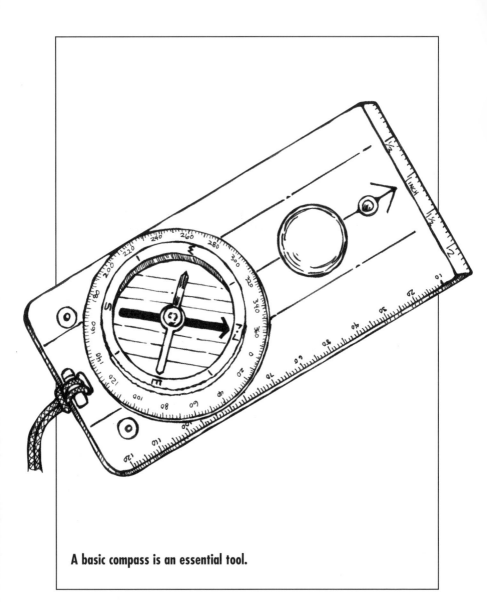

A basic compass is an essential tool.

and structures like powerlines or buildings. Contour lines connect areas of similar elevation to show you how the ground is shaped. Contour lines that are very close together indicate a steep area, like a cliff, while lines that are spaced farther apart represent flatter regions.

Map stores, map companies, ranger stations, visitor centers, outfitting stores, and government agencies are all good sources for topographic maps. Also look for kiosks at popular national parks and large outfitting stores for a software program that allows you to print a color topo map of the exact region you plan to visit. This program was developed by a partnership between National Geographic and the United States Geological Survey (USGS). Instead of piecing together various USGS quads, this mapping program allows you to zero in on the region relevant to your trip so that you walk away with one map that shows the exact area you'll be hiking in.

Before you leave home, use your map to locate water sources and potential campsites. Become familiar with your route and notice where the trail climbs or descends steeply or where it crosses a river. Determine how far it is to landmarks along your route. For example, how many miles is it from the trailhead to the first water source? Familiarizing yourself with the region through which you'll be hiking is the first step toward staying found.

The second step is to refer to your map frequently throughout your trip. Do the trail signs make sense? Do the landmarks you see on the trail correspond to those on the map? If everything checks out, try using a compass to further your orienteering skills. A basic compass will serve all your navigation needs. Start by finding the direction in which you're traveling. Hold the compass flat in your palm with the direction-of-travel arrow pointing in the direction you're heading. Rotate the compass housing until the red end of the magnetic needle is aligned with the orienting needle. (Think "red in the shed" to remember this.) The direction you're traveling (measured in degrees and referred to as a bearing) will be at the top of the dial.

Walking a bearing is likely the most valuable compass skill to master. This technique is useful when you know where you want to go but when your destination is obstructed along the route. For example, from the clearing where you're standing you see the ridgeline that you want to get to, but you have to walk through a dense forest to get there. If you set a bearing, you can head straight toward the ridge even when you can't see it.

Give it a try. You can practice this anywhere, even in your backyard. Stand outside and face an object that you want to walk toward, like a big tree. Hold the compass in the palm of your hand and point the direction-of-travel arrow at the tree. Turn the compass housing until red end of the magnetic needle is aligned with the orienting arrow. Read the bearing on the dial. If you walk that bearing you will end up at the tree.

When you're far away from your destination, pick an object that is in line with your bearing and walk toward it. When you get there, take another sighting along the bearing you've been walking and walk toward it. Eventually you'll arrive at your destination.

Solo Hiking

Trails are often marked with stripes of paint, called blazes, that appear on trees and rocks along the route.

To improve your compass skills, contact your local community center, outdoor club, or parks and recreation department for clinics and classes, or take a look at one of the numerous books that have been written on this subject.

Route Finding

One of the biggest responsibilities for the solo traveler is to pay attention to where you're going and where you've been. It's easy to let your mind wander and lose yourself to the rhythm of your footfalls and the enormity of an unspoiled landscape. By all means enjoy the walk, but don't neglect your safety. Every quarter mile or so, make a written or mental note of where you are and how you feel. Are you still on the right trail? Can you tell where your route goes? Is the terrain still within

Routes through treeless areas are often marked with piles of rocks called cairns.

your ability level? Pay attention to landmarks like valleys, ridges, streams, and peculiar rock formations. If you have to backtrack it will be helpful if you can recollect the exact route you came from.

In addition to maintaining a general awareness of land features and a general idea of how far you've come, pay particular attention to trail markers. Trails are generally marked with emblems or paint stripes called blazes. Routes through treeless regions are often signed with posts or with piles of rocks called cairns. If ever you come upon a confusing junction or an unclear route, stop and consult your map. You should be able to spot the next post or cairn from the previous one. If you don't see it immediately, stop and scan the area. Never wander aimlessly in search of your route. The most important thing for the soloist to remember is to pay attention to the map, to the landscape, to your mileage, and to landmarks and signage.

Solo Hiking   **45**

River Crossings

Crossing rivers is an inherently dangerous part of hiking, and it's even more dangerous when you're traveling by yourself. When you're with others it is possible to form a chain and support your partners when crossing, and it is somewhat reassuring to know that if you do fall, your partners may be able to help you out. The soloist doesn't have these luxuries.

On many trail systems, bodies of water are bridged. It's always a good idea to inquire at a local ranger station whether waterways are bridged with sturdy structures or by a single log. If you don't feel comfortable balancing on a log, especially one that may be narrow or slippery, you may want to ask about other options or other routes.

If your route involves a ford—that is, a river that's not bridged—you will have to decide if crossing the river is within your comfort and ability levels. A shallow stream may be crossed by stepping from rock to rock, but beware! Even the smallest streams can be dangerous if you slip, and normally quiet creeks can rage after a heavy rain. Do not take river crossings lightly; treat *all* water with respect.

Should you decide to ford a river, the technique you'll use is the same for rivers of any depth. First, walk along the bank to scout the crossing. Toss softball-sized rocks into the water to determine how deep it is. A hollow "kerplunk!" indicates deeper water. If the river is braided into a number of channels, find the widest, shallowest parts of the river. Usually the more narrow the channel, the swifter the current.

Before you get your feet wet, unclasp your hip belt and loosen the straps. If you end up going for a swim, it will be important to be able to easily slip out of the pack so that it doesn't pull you under. A hiking stick or a pair of trekking poles will be quite helpful; they provide considerable stability during a crossing. For long crossings, crossings in very cold water, or crossings where the stream bottom may be especially sharp or slippery, I cross in my hiking boots; otherwise I change into sandals or old sneakers and keep my boots dry. Avoid crossing in bare feet; rocks and debris can cut your feet, and bare feet don't offer much traction on mossy rocks.

As you cross, focus on the opposite shore—avoid looking down into the current, as the rush of water will likely make you dizzy. Step slowly and carefully. Make sure each step is stable and supported before you lift the other foot.

Keep in mind that water levels in many mountain streams are lower in the morning and get higher as the afternoon sun melts snow and funnels water into the riverbeds.

If at any time you are apprehensive about a crossing, it may be

When fording a river, wear sturdy footwear, use trekking poles for balance, and don't be afraid to turn around if the current is swifter than you anticipated.

wise to select an alternate route or return the way you came. When confronted with a challenging crossing it is better to play it safe than risk going for a swim. Don't feel badly about aborting a ford—we all do it from time to time.

Staying Healthy

On any backcountry excursion a variety of factors exist that could jeopardize your safety. In the following sections we'll talk about environmental risks like cold weather and bears; injuries like sprained ankles; and precautions to take to avoid unfavorable encounters with people, especially during hunting season. Potential threats to the solo hiker may seem plentiful, but think about a similar list for your day-to-day life. The risks we're exposed to when living in towns or cities far outnumber those associated with backcountry travel. While the odds of something happening to you are slim, it's best to be prepared and do all you can to prevent injury and illness. As a soloist it is much easier to prevent or avoid problems than it is to get out of trouble once you're in it.

Environmental Risks

WEATHER

The most obvious environmental risk is inclement weather. Because the signs and symptoms associated with illness caused by both hot and cold temperatures can be subtle and difficult to detect, it is very important for the soloist to frequently monitor his or her condition. Expect and prepare for extreme conditions on all your backcountry outings.

HYPOTHERMIA

When you encounter cold, wet, or windy conditions, your body tries to compensate for heat loss by reducing blood flow to your extremities (which reduces heat loss to the environment) and by shivering (which generates heat). When the cold overwhelms your body's ability to compensate, you become hypothermic. Understand that a hypothermic condition can be aggravated by wind, rain, and exhaustion and can occur in temperatures as warm as 50 degrees. Hypothermia can creep up on you if you're just a little cold for a long period of time, so the symptoms are often difficult to recognize. If you are shivering, start to mumble, experience numbness, and feel tired, you are probably becoming hypothermic. You'll need to correct the condition immediately before it progresses to a more severe state. Treat hypothermia by getting into warm, dry clothes, eating, and exercising. Be careful to balance exercising with eating: If your body runs out of fuel, your condition will quickly deteriorate. As a hypothermic condition worsens, shivering will cease and you may lose consciousness.

Especially when you're alone, be sensitive to your need to stay warm. Bundle up before you become chilled, store your sleeping bag and extra clothes in waterproof sacks, and stay well fed and hydrated. In an emergency, it may be helpful to climb into your tent and light a candle. Even a small flame will heat a tent's interior and will help dry out your clothes. Just be careful with the flame, as most tents are highly flammable.

HEAT-RELATED ILLNESS

On the other end of the spectrum is heat-related illness. If you hike in hot weather, be aware that your body will be working very hard to keep your core body temperature around 98.6 degrees Fahrenheit. Your body will cool as you sweat and as the moisture evaporates from your

A sunhat, sunglasses, and tank top are good items to wear in very hot weather. And don't forget the sunscreen!

Solo Hiking 49

skin. Humidity of the air and exposure to wind can affect your body's natural cooling process. In dry, windy conditions the cooling process is more efficient, but in still, humid weather it becomes much more difficult to stay cool.

A sure sign that your body is no longer able to deal with the heat effectively is painful muscle spasms in your legs or abdomen. If not treated immediately, your heat-related illness can progress to heat exhaustion. In this condition, your skin may become either pale or flushed and your breathing will be rapid and shallow. You may also feel dizzy, weak, nauseated, and have a headache. If you acquire any of these symptoms, take action immediately. Especially when you're on your own, it is important to continually give yourself the once-over; check in with yourself and evaluate how you're feeling. If you feel that you're overheating, stop hiking immediately. Find a shady spot to rest, elevate your feet, and sip water. If you're near water, wet a bandanna and make a cold compress. Don't continue until your symptoms subside; if you are severely dehydrated, a condition that precipitates heat exhaustion, it may take more than twelve hours to fully recover.

When you're traveling in hot environments, it's important to dress for the occasion. Wear light cotton clothing, a sunhat, sunglasses, and sunscreen. Drink continuously, and eat salty snacks to replace electrolytes lost through sweat. Avoid hiking in the middle of the day, and take frequent rest breaks.

LIGHTNING

Lightning is the number one weather-related killer in the United States and is a real danger to backcountry travelers. Anyone who has been close to a lightning strike can attest to just how terrifying an experience it is. While the best tactic for dealing with an electrical storm is avoidance, sometimes there's nothing you can do to avoid a storm; you'll have to depend on a combination of smart thinking and good luck to get you through it.

You're on your own for the luck part of the equation, but I can give you some advice on strategies that will decrease your odds of being struck. First, lightning has an affinity for tall objects, water, and metal, so stay away from all three. That means move downhill, off ridges and mountaintops, away from lakes and solitary trees. If the storm is very close and getting struck by lightning seems a real possibility, remove your backpack and walk away from it. Metal components in your backpack and tent become dangerous in an electrical storm. Also, as tempting as it seems, don't crawl into a shallow cave; lightning will move easily across the mouth of a cave, and if you're in it's path, you'll be struck, too. The rule is that if the depth of the cave is three times

In a severe electrical storm, take off your backpack and assume the lightning-safe position.

that of its mouth, then it's probably safe. Your best bet, however, is to move into a dense stand of trees of relatively similar height. Move to a low elevation if possible. Again, if the possibility of a strike seems great (for example, if the hair on your body is standing on end), remove your pack and squat down on your sleeping mattress so that only the soles of your boots are touching the mattress. Although it's difficult to test the effectiveness of this stance, it has been dubbed the "lightning-safe position."

AVALANCHE

When traveling solo, all avalanche conditions should be avoided. The risks are high: If you get caught in an avalanche, nobody will be there to get you out. If you travel through areas where avalanche conditions exist (such as high-mountain regions in spring), it is a good idea to take an avalanche awareness course and learn how to assess the likelihood of avalanche in current snow conditions.

Solo Hiking   **51**

Animals

On one hand, soloists are at an advantage when dealing with wildlife because we tend to be more aware of our surroundings. We may pay better attention to sounds in the backcountry and may be more careful where we step and where we place our hands. On the other hand, when it comes to large mammals like bears or mountain lions, we are clearly at a disadvantage. A group certainly has a better chance of fending off aggressive wildlife, scaring it away, and alerting wildlife to human presence so as not to startle an unsuspecting critter.

In this section we'll talk about bears, snakes, and spiders; however, the list of potentially dangerous animals doesn't end there. Consider ticks, alligators, mountain lions, wolves, javelinas, moose, and domestic cattle. Inquire at a ranger station or visitor center about potentially dangerous animals that inhabit the area through which you'll be hiking. Especially when you venture into unfamiliar territory, it is a good idea to become educated about local wildlife. Learn what the animal's tracks look like, what type of habitat it prefers, and measures you can take to avoid conflict.

BEARS

Common throughout most parts of North America, the black bear may be the animal most feared by hikers. While most populations of black bears maintain a fear of humans, some bears, especially those that have gotten human food, may be bold and act aggressively. If you're hiking through bear country, be on the lookout for the bruins, and never approach one if you see it.

The most dangerous situations you can be in with a bear are surprising one or coming between a sow and her cubs. Avoid these situations by staying alert and by making noise to alert bears to your presence. In bear country, hikers often attach small bells to their backpacks; however, recent research has shown that bears perceived these "bear bells" as normal background noise. Indeed, to a bear the tinkling of bells can sound like birds chirping, water trickling, or leaves rustling—not an approaching human. The best way to alert a bear to your presence is to use the instrument that is uniquely human: your voice. No doubt this is a challenging task when you're by yourself. At first you may feel self-conscious talking or singing to yourself, but don't let that stop you. It's better to receive a strange look from a passing hiker than an angry look from Mama Bear. You may also find it difficult to keep speaking on long uphill climbs; usually my song deteriorates into fragmented lyrics separated by gasps for breath! Do your best, rest frequently, and stay alert.

Usually when hikers see bears they do so from a distance and the bear usually turns and scoots into the woods. If you see a bear, even in the distance (say, more than 100 yards away), don't approach it. Wait until it leaves the area, or alter your course to avoid getting closer. If you come upon a bear at close range, stop immediately and let the bear know you're human by speaking calmly and loudly and by waving your arms above your head. No other animal waves its arms like humans do, so right away the bear should perceive you as something different. Slowly back away from the bear. At this point, the bear will usually recognize you as human and leave you alone. However, if a grizzly perceives you as a threat, it may bluff charge you—that is, the bear will run at you and either stop short or veer away. As scary as this sounds, it is imperative that you stand still and hold your ground. If a grizzly

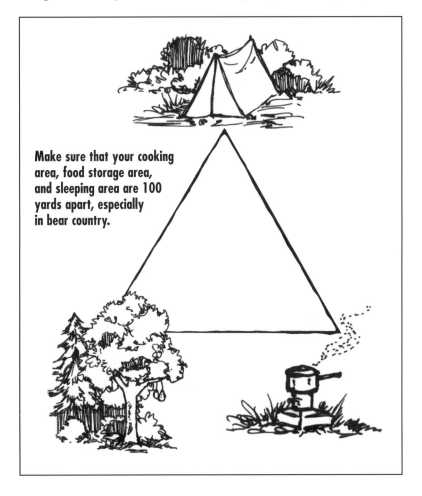

Make sure that your cooking area, food storage area, and sleeping area are 100 yards apart, especially in bear country.

makes contact with you, drop to the ground in fetal position and play dead. If a black bear attacks you, fight back with your hiking stick, knife, rocks, or with whatever you can. Under no circumstance should you drop your backpack and run. You cannot outrun a bear, and if a bear gets a food reward, it will quickly learn to associate humans with food and will repeat its behavior on the next hiker.

When camping in bear country it's important to select a campsite with good visibility so that you can see a bear approaching. It's also imperative to maintain a clean camp and be able to quickly pack up your food. Avoid spreading out all your groceries. If a bear approaches, pack up quickly, take your food, and move away from the area. Store food in a bear-resistant food container or a bear locker, or hang it on a bear pole (see page 18 for other food storage techniques). These facilities are often provided at campsites in bear country. It's a good idea to store all scented items like toothpaste and insect repellent with your food. I make sure my entire hygiene kit, trash bag, and all my cookware are stored a good distance from my tent. To a bear these smells may be perceived as interesting, and a curious bear will want to investigate the smell to find out if it tastes good.

To maintain a safe camp, make a triangle between your tent site, cooking area, and food storage area, making sure they are 100 yards apart. Keep your equipment and clothing as clean as possible; pick up any spilled pasta or dropped peanuts.

Some hikers feel more comfortable in bear country with a can of pepper spray in a holster on their hip. Research has shown that pepper spray often deters a curious bear if the bear is hit directly in the face. However, its effectiveness is questionable in the face of an aggressive bear, and at least some people think that pepper spray is likely to aggravate the bear even further. The effectiveness of this deterrent is debatable, and it's a personal choice whether you choose to carry it. Also consider that pepper spray is a food item (it's made primarily from cayenne pepper) and should be stored away from your tent at night.

If you know you'll be passing through areas with high densities of bears, with particularly aggressive bears, or with grizzly bears (in pockets of the northwestern contiguous United States, Canada, and Alaska), you may want to rethink going solo. Solo travel in most parts of Alaska, for example, is highly discouraged because it's very difficult to make enough noise and keep a watchful eye out for bears when you're by yourself.

SNAKES

Poisonous snakes can be found in most of the United States. Of the four venomous snakes found in North America, the rattlesnake is most common. The cottonmouth, or water moccasin, is found largely in southeastern swamps. Copperheads may be encountered in the East, and the coral snake resides in the Southeast and Southwest. Snakes typically prefer to rest under logs and rocks, and, like all creatures, they get nervous when threatened or cornered. It's our responsibility to avoid putting a snake in that situation.

The first step is to know when you're hiking in an area that is home to a venomous snake. The second step is to watch where you place your hands and feet. As you reach for a rock to catch your balance, be aware that you may be reaching into a snake's home and that your gesture is probably not welcome. I like to wear sturdy boots and gaiters when I'm hiking in snake country. It makes me feel better to know that if my step startles a snake, the striking serpent will have a heck of a time getting through a piece of leather.

In the unlikely event that a venomous snake bites you, realize that only about half of snakebites contain venom. If the bite is poisonous, you may experience stinging pain, severe burning, nausea, weakness, rapid pulse, and labored breathing. There is nothing you can do in the field; you must seek medical help immediately to receive the appropriate antivenin. Don't waste time cutting yourself, soaking the bite in cold water, or applying a tourniquet—these are all ineffective techniques. Get yourself to a medical facility as quickly as possible.

SPIDERS

Of the three types of dangerously venomous spiders in the United States, the black widow (a black spider with a red hourglass marking on its underside) is most common. It is found throughout the country, especially in the East and California. The brown recluse (a light brown spider with a darker brown, violin-shaped marking on its back) can be found in the Midwest and in parts of the South, and other recluse spiders reside in the Southwest. The hobo spider makes its home in the Northwest.

All three like dark, hidden places and will respond the same way a snake will when cornered or threatened—they'll bite. So be especially careful where you place your hands when you're in an outhouse, when you're scrambling over rocks, or when you're gathering firewood for a campfire.

If you're bitten by a venomous spider you may experience stinging pain, cramps, nausea, or flulike symptoms. If you are bitten, seek medical help immediately. If you can describe to a doctor the type of spider that bit you, it will expedite the recovery process, as the doctor will be able to prescribe the correct antivenin to counteract the poison.

Solo Hiking   **55**

If you meet another hiker, send that person for help and try to keep still (this will slow down the spread of poison throughout your body). Encourage bleeding to get rid of the venom, then apply a cold, wet bandanna to the bite. Keep the affected area below your heart if possible.

Injuries

Minor injuries like a blister, a sprained ankle, or a cut on your hand must be carefully dealt with no matter where you are, but injuries to the solo hiker warrant extra considerations. That is because there is no one else to tend to your wounds, to help you walk, to go for help, or to make good decisions if your judgment becomes impaired. Even minor injuries can pose a serious threat to the soloist, and a serious injury can quickly become a serious problem. In this section we'll talk about treating common injuries and dealing with incapacitating ones when you're on your own.

But first, a few words about prevention. A friend of mine, who is a highly skilled mountain climber, can be found nearly every weekend scaling some formidable peak or traversing a seemingly impassable ridgeline. One time I asked her how she has the nerve to do what she does. I asked her if she ever gets scared. She told me that before she attempts something dangerous she weighs the risks and rewards and thinks about the worst-case scenario. If she believes she can live with the worst-case scenario (which might be, for example, falling from a 10-foot ledge), then she continues with the activity. In the course of a day she might evaluate twenty different risky situations, and one by one she gets through them either by proceeding through the obstacle or by finding an alternate route.

You might try something similar. In any potentially risky situation (a stretch of rocky terrain, a river crossing, a ridge with a lot of exposure, or an approaching storm, for example), evaluate the risks and consider the possible consequences of your actions. Know that it's okay to back away and opt for the safer alternative.

When you're out there, rest often and stop before you get so tired that you're no longer paying attention to where you're stepping. Stay well fed and well hydrated and you'll be less likely to become injured. Careless mistakes are often made when hikers become fatigued.

Take other preventive measures before you leave home. Enroll in a first-aid course at your local fire department, or take an advanced wilderness medicine course from a reputable organization like Stonehearth Open Learning Opportunities (603-447-6711; www.stonehearth. com); the Wilderness Medicine Institute

(970-641-3572; www.wildernessmed.com); or Wilderness Medical Associates (888-945-3633; www.wildmed.com).

Another preventive measure is to live a healthy lifestyle by staying drug-free, eating nutritious meals, managing stress, and staying fit and flexible.

Before you set out on a hiking trip you may want to get your body used to hiking and carrying a backpack. Start small and increase the length of your trips and the weight of your pack. The better shape you're in, the less time you'll need to prepare your body for the rigors of backpacking.

Even if you're already in good shape, it's still a good idea to get accustomed to walking on uneven terrain and sporting a heavy pack, for these are things that even good athletes might not be used to. It's also important to stay flexible. Stretching before and after exercise decreases your chance of getting injured; long, loose muscles will respond faster and make you less susceptible to strains and sprains.

BLISTERS

Blisters are likely the most common backcountry injury. A blister is essentially a burn. It's caused by friction-generated heat. Your boots and socks rub against your skin and soon you have what we call a hot spot, a very tender red area. A blister will appear when the hot spot is not treated and fills with fluid. The trick is to treat hot spots before they become blisters. Pad the area around the hot spot to reduce friction on the affected area. Try not to put the bandage directly over the hot spot; that may not be very comfortable.

A protective covering like moleskin should be part of every hiker's first-aid kit. Before I leave home I cut holes in the center of moleskin squares so that when I'm in the field my bandages are ready to go. I like to pad the area around the hot spot with a doughnut-shaped covering then put a Band-Aid over top. This way the Band-Aid doesn't actually touch the hot spot but helps keep the area clean. Experiment with moleskin, Molefoam, and other blister coverings to find one that works well for you.

If you continue to walk on a hot spot that has filled with fluid, expect the blister to rupture. When this happens, clean the area thoroughly, apply an antibiotic ointment, cover it with a sterile dressing, and monitor for signs of infection. A local infection, which appears red and sometimes pussy, ought to be treated as soon as possible (and may involve taking antibiotics). If you see red streaks radiating from the wound, you may have a systemic infection, which can be life threatening. Seek medical help immediately.

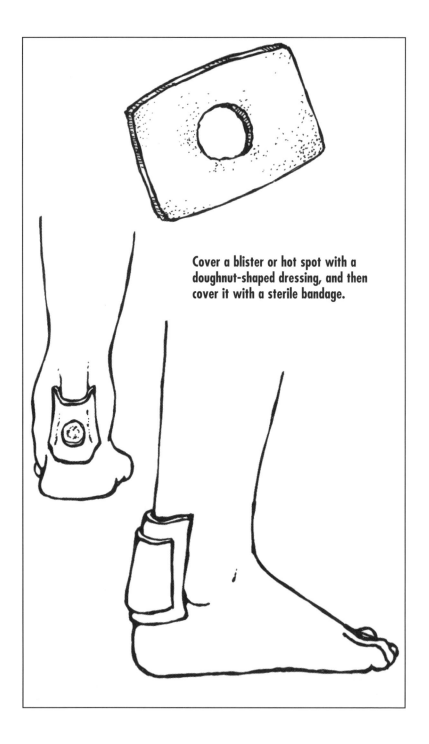

Cover a blister or hot spot with a doughnut-shaped dressing, and then cover it with a sterile bandage.

If you do develop a full-blown blister, evaluate the situation. How much pain is it causing you? Will it have a chance to heal during your trip? You may want to consider shortening your trip or scheduling a rest day to give your blister a chance to heal. Blisters, as small and as insignificant as they may seem, can become incapacitating if left untreated.

WOUNDS

Wounds like cuts and scrapes occur quite frequently in the back-country. You may brush up against a rock, get poked by a tree limb, or stumble over a root. Minor wounds should be cleaned immediately with treated water and dressed with a sterile bandage to prevent infection. If the wound is more than a minor scrape and if you are bleeding severely, your first priority is to stop the bleeding. Cover the wound with a sterile dressing or a clean T-shirt or bandanna, and apply pressure to the wound. If blood soaks through, do not remove the dressing; instead, put more layers on top of the blood-soaked ones and continue to apply pressure.

The solo hiker needs to be extra careful when making a decision whether to continue on. If you think a minor injury may get worse, it's better to make your way to a road than risk having your condition deteriorate when you're by yourself in the wilderness.

SPRAINED ANKLE

It happens so quickly. One minute you're happily bouncing down the trail; the next, you've tweaked your ankle on a rock and can hardly

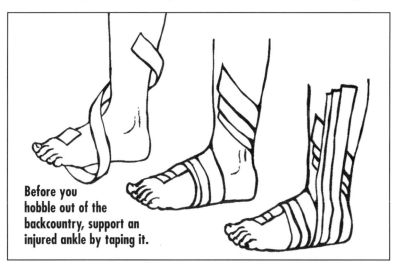

Before you hobble out of the backcountry, support an injured ankle by taping it.

stand up. The first thing you must do is stop and evaluate how bad the injury is. If you heard a snap or a pop or if you cannot put any weight on the ankle, sit tight, you're not going anywhere. If you feel as though it's a minor sprain (which, technically, is a stretch injury to the ligament), soak your ankle in a cold stream and elevate it. Before you hobble out, wrap the ankle with an elastic bandage or tape it to make it more stable. If you've injured your ankle on a solo trip it is best to hobble out as soon as you can. Swelling will commence, which may make it quite difficult and painful to wear a hiking boot, and the injury will likely get worse before it feels better. Grab a couple of hiking sticks and make your way to medical help as soon as possible.

Signaling and Rescues

If you have a more severe injury, such as a severe sprain, a dislocation, or a fracture, it may be practically impossible to hobble your way to medical help. Here is where the danger of going solo is most apparent. Depending on where you're hiking, you may cross paths with another hiker who can call for help. If not, you may have some important decisions to make: (1) Stay put, signal for help, and wait to be rescued, or (2) jury-rig a splint and crutches and make your way out. In some instances even the most well-constructed crutches will not help you get very far. If your injury is severe you may have no choice but to wait for help to come to you. Consider that the rescue process will be expedited if you left an itinerary with rangers or family. When you don't return, they will initiate a search and hopefully know where to look to find you.

There are a number of universal signals for help. Blowing a whistle in three short blows will alert other hikers or rescuers to your location. Using a small mirror to reflect the sun may alert aircraft to your presence. Building a smoky fire may alert rescuers to your whereabouts. Most important, be patient. It may take time to find you. Treat your injury the best way you know how, stay well fed and hydrated, and keep warm. This will greatly increase your chance of survival.

A note about search and rescue. This is a service that is typically composed of volunteers. Rescues often involve tremendous risk to the rescuers. Rescues are also extremely expensive. For these reasons and many others, signal for help only when you really need it. There have been a number of instances where tired, cold, and only mildly injured hikers have demanded a helicopter rescue when they could have walked out on their own.

Other People

A significant number of hikers are deterred from going solo because they are afraid of other people. This is certainly a legitimate concern, especially for solo women, who may be more vulnerable to an attack. It comes down to this: If a good portion of your time in the backcountry will be spent feeling afraid and alone, you may want to rethink going solo. If you acknowledge that there are risks and are comfortable accepting those risks, then you will likely have an enjoyable experience.

There are certain things that no amount of forethought or training will prevent, and that applies to many situations in many different places, not just to backcountry attacks. We must be willing to accept some degree of risk; else we would never do anything.

I'd like to focus on measures you can take to discourage a potential attacker from pursuing you. First, don't tell strangers your exact itinerary and don't feel obligated to disclose more information about your trip than you're comfortable sharing. When I walk down the trail, even on dayhikes, it is not uncommon for people to ask me if I'm alone. Usually I have a good feeling about the people who ask; they seem concerned about my well-being or simply interested in what I'm doing. But now and again something about the question rubs me the wrong way and I tell them, "No, my friends are on their way," and glance behind me as if expecting them to round the corner. I continue on and figure that by the time they realize I am indeed traveling solo, I'll be far away.

When asked where I'll camp, I usually say I haven't yet decided where I'll spend the night. Use your common sense: If a person makes you feel the least bit uncomfortable, don't stick around. Depending on your comfort level, either continue on your way or head to an area where it's likely you'll run into other people.

In fact, just because you're going solo doesn't mean you have to deny yourself all contact with other hikers. It can be quite enjoyable and comforting to travel on regularly used trails and stay at popular campsites. Especially on your first few solo outings, you may feel more at ease knowing that others are nearby. It's a good combination: You have other hikers around you in case you get into trouble, but you still don't have to share your sleeping space with a snoring tentmate!

It's also not a bad idea to give the impression that you're camping with others. At camp you can make it look like there's more than one of you by spreading out your gear and putting your hiking boots and camp shoes by the tent door.

Hunting Season

While I'm rarely afraid of a premeditated attack, my guard is always raised during hunting season. The possibility that an inexperienced hunter will mistake me for game weighs heavily on my mind. During popular seasons, it may be prudent to stay out of the woods altogether or to choose a location that's closed to hunting.

If you do venture out with the hunters, there are a number of things you can do to decrease the likelihood of an accident. First, find out when hunting seasons occur. Learn which animals are being hunted and learn where those animals live—then avoid those areas. Wear blaze orange and stick to main trails. It's also a good idea to make noise to alert hunters to the fact that you are a person, not a deer, moving through the woods.

Appendix

Resources

Berger, Karen. *Everyday Wisdom: 1,001 Expert Tips for Hikers.* Mountaineers Books. 1997.

Davidson, Robyn. *From Alice to Ocean: Alone Across the Outback.* Addison-Wesley. 1994.

Davidson, Robyn. *Tracks: A Woman's Solo Trek Across 1700 Miles of Australian Outback.* Vintage Books. 1995.

Ehlers, Karl F. *Solo Safe! A Guide to Safe Backcountry Travel for the Individual.* Buffalo Press. 2000.

Hall, Adrienne. *A Journey North: One Woman's Story of Hiking the Appalachian Trail.* Appalachian Mountain Club. 2001.

Jardine, Ray. *Beyond Backpacking: Ray Jardine's Guide to Lightweight Hiking.* Adventure Lore Press. 1999.

McManners, Hugh. *101 Essential Tips: Hiking.* DK Publishing. 1998.

Rogers, Susan Fox. *Solo: On Her Own Adventure.* Seal Press. 1996.

Ross, Cindy. *A Hiker's Companion: 12,000 Miles of Trail-Tested Wisdom.* Mountaineers Books. 1993.

Shaffer, Earl V. *The Appalachian Trail: Calling Me Back to the Hills.* Westcliffe. 2001.

Shaffer, Earl V. *Walking with Spring.* Appalachian Trail Conference. 1983.

Townsend, Chris. *Crossing Arizona: A Solo Hike through the Sky Islands and Deserts of the Arizona Trail.* Countryman Press. 2002.

Townsend, Chris. *Walking the Yukon: A Solo Trek through the Land of Beyond.* Tab Books. 1993.

MT. LEBANON PUBLIC LIBRARY

Appendix

Zero-Impact Guidelines

◆ Pack out everything you pack in (including wrappers, apple cores, and toilet paper).

◆ Stay on the trail. Don't cut switchbacks or widen the trail in any way.

◆ Do not feed or harass wildlife, and do not disturb cultural sites.

◆ Never put soap in a water source. Clean clothes, cookware, and do all bathing at least 200 feet from a water source.

◆ Camp at least 200 feet from a water source and refrain from trampling sensitive vegetation around water sources.

◆ Bury human waste in a hole 4 to 8 inches deep and at least 200 feet from a water source.

◆ Refrain from using technology (such as a cell phone or laptop computer) around other hikers.

Index

About the Author

Adrienne Hall holds a bachelor's degree in biology and a masters in environmental studies. She is author of *A Journey North: One Women's Story of Hiking the Appalachian Trail, A Woman's Guide to Backpacking,* and *The Essential Backpacker.* She lives in Anchorage, Alaska.

MT. LEBANON PUBLIC LIBRARY